POEMS
NEW, USED,
AND REBUILDS

JEFF VANDE ZANDE

Copyright © 2007
Jeff Vande Zande
March Street Press
3413 Wilshire
Greensboro NC 27408-2923
http://www.marchstreetpress.com
rbixby@earthlink.net
fax 336 282 9754
isbn 1-59661-078-6

Cover photo by Michael Randolph

Thank you to the editors of the following magazines in which some of these poems first appeared:

Asphodel, Birmingham Poetry Review, Blue Collar Review, The Bridge, Controlled Burn, Crab Creek Review, Fugue, Green Hills Literary Lantern, Karamu, Main Street Rag, Midwest Poetry Review, New American Imagist, The Oakland Journal, Parting Gifts, Passages North, Pearl, Rattle, Remark, River Oak Review, and *Sulphur River Literary Review.*

College English "She Chose to Wade" Copyright 1998 National Council of Teachers of English. Reprinted with permission.

Poems in this collection also appeared, sometimes in different versions, in the following chapbooks: *Last Name First, First Name Last* (Partisan Press), *Transient* (March Street Press), and *Tornado Warning* (March Street Press).

"Blood Work" appeared in *Family Matters: Poems of Our Families,* an anthology by Bottom Dog Press.

"Clean" also was selected to appear in Poet Laureate Ted Kooser's nationally syndicated newspaper column, American Life in Poetry.

Cover photo by Michael Randolph.

Still Life   1
After Two Weeks   2
Fixing   4
Transient   5
Night Travel   6
Carpooling   7
Punched Out   8
After Seeing the Specialist in Detroit   10
Highways Up North   12
Labor Day Weekend   13
The Survivalist   15
Something We Must Face   18
Fishing Weekend, Seven Hours North of Detroit   20
Gestures   21
Snowfall   22
South Michigan Interstate, Near Detroit   25
Only Birds After All   27
A Bus   29
Road Signs   31
Tornado Warning   32
Below Zero   34
My Father Wrote Short Stories   35
Broken Lamoge   37
Pretend Water   38
Back Casting, Forward Casting   39
Last Cutting Before Snow   41
Toddler Classes   43
Driving Home from a Niece's Funeral   45
Alternate Weekend: Eclipse   47
She Chose to Wade   48
Survival Tactics   50
Reprieve   52
Up into the Light   54
Sundown   56
Losing Work   58

Summer Shutdowns   60
Breakdown   62
How it happens   63
Flotsam and Jetsam   65
The Other   67
Opening   69
Green   70
Clean   72
Sleep Over   74
Blood Work   76
Another Man Admires My Wife's Cups   79
What We Have   81
Stripped   84
Epiphany   86

Still Life

Home from his third twelve-hour shift
he stoops down into the cold fridge,
his back slow like a rusty hinge.

Behind him, the sliding glass door
is both a window and a mirror,
dark and light against the pane.

Ghostly, his reflection floats
among the silhouettes of leafless trees,
their limbs splintering through him.

Rootless, his feet are nearly dissolved
in both snow and linoleum.
An empty bird feeder hangs in his rib cage.

He decides he's too tired to eat,
closes the door, hands empty,
and walks into the dark living room.

After Two Weeks

*I can't sleep
without the ocean
hushing in my ears.*
My daughter tells me this,
midnight, her tiny silhouette
in the doorway to our bedroom.
Go back to bed, sweety I finally say,
remembering that my wife
is back on third shift.

I can't sleep either,
not in this bed,
not without the numbness,
not without the dull hum
of the drill press
resonating in my bones.
Tomorrow I'll punch in again.
The alarm is set for six.

The man I became on the beach,
the man who studied the insides
of a washed-up jellyfish
for nearly an hour,
the man who finishes sentences
with *sweety*,
will lie down

for me to bore holes through,
one after another after a thousand
until there's nothing left,
until, in a few weeks,
I'll be able to sleep again
like the dead.

Fixing

Despite my hammer
and my rolled sleeves,
he crosses the road.
When I started this morning,
boys in the neighborhood
thought it was another gun.
Still, he crosses my lawn,
says his full name,
and slips his fingers and thumb
over my palm like a wrench,
as though this handshaking
were tightening something.
He walks home with a socket
in his pocket, thanks me again.
In July, he'll help me
knock apart an old fence
that's choking off the lilac bushes.
For now, I sink another nail
into our front porch.

Carpooling

A voice from the backseat
gathers like a dream
into their sleepy commute.

*Just look at how
many shades of green* she says,
her head nodding
toward the trees in the median.

The driver turns
his eyes out of the lines,
witnesses how the wind
moves like fingers
under a blouse of leaves,
emerald, olive, jade, lime…

Too soon, he'll wake
to the morning's first backup:
monotony of brake lights,
the backseat dwindling
into gossip.

Punched Out

Punched out, off the line,
he speeds into the vague promise
of the interstate, blacktop
in touch with any other place,

even the northern cities
his bosses own land around,
Charlevoix, Petoskey, East Jordan,
destinations only three hours away
according to the vow of green signs.

He wonders if he will burst
into wings on the main street
of Traverse City, like a nymph
opens into mayfly at the surface
of the Au Sable river.

His exit fades in the rearview mirror,
and he doesn't recognize his own
dilated pupils staring back at him.
He wonders if the hunger he feels
is just the dinner he hasn't cooked.

A June bug, like a calloused finger,
taps its death against the windshield.
Something in its mad swoop toward
the light tells him his engine's
A to B miles shouldn't be wasted.

Turning back, he lets the white
dashes hypnotize him until television
and then sleep. Before dawn
he will find himself again
on the line, punched in.

After Seeing the Specialist in Detroit

The father and son drive into darkness
north along the Lake Huron shoreline.
The waves below break against the beaches.
In the passenger seat, leaned against the window,
the father stares at the high beams
shattering through long stands of trees,
empty limbs gathered into blackness.
Hands on the wheel, ten and two,
the son keeps the car between the lines.
A sign flashes by—silhouette of a buck
bounding across a yellow field.
The father closes his eyes.
> *You never swerve*
> *if one springs in front of the car,*
> *too good a chance you'll smash*
> *into oncoming traffic, or end up*
> *totaled in the ditch, then insurance*
> *won't pay for shit.*

The son watches the dark shoulders.
> *Don't hit the brakes, or the front end*
> *dips and lifts two hundred pounds*
> *of venison up through the windshield.*

The father yawns and reclines
out of sight, leaves his son alone
above the dashboard. *Hit the gas.*

If you're going to hit it, kill it.
Otherwise, it lies all twisted
in the long grass and just twitches.
He rolls on his side, back
towards the driver's seat, coughs
his way down into sleep.
The road coils out of night
into the half light of the high beams.
Alone, the son clenches the wheel,
watches the edges, ready for anything.

Highways Up North

Beyond the guard rails
tiny windows burn
like pilot lights: ice shanties
huddled together on a lake.
Fishermen park on the water
and twist their augers down.
During the long stretches,
they knock on each other's doors,
share coffee, chili, whiskey.
Occasionally, their shouts echo
above the highway moaning
as they lure shimmering life
from cold, dark holes.

Labor Day Weekend

Drifting through dark houses, fathers rattle
doorknobs and startle their families awake.

Outside, they check hitches and safety chains,
their trailers loaded with motorcycles

or boats, everything they'll need to speed
or float deeper into the meaning of things.

Their families stumble out, yawning,
but ready to follow a sliver of headlights

into the long miles of blackness,
always north, always away from cities

towards two-tracks and dirt roads
where rivers and trails wind out

into acres of birch and evergreen.
Broken out of cabin doors, lap dogs will run

into clear-cut fields and flush the thrum
of partridge from under young cedars.

Bon fires will leap
into the darkness, and the shadows

of the slightest gestures will dance
high and wild in the tree tops

as though the motion of a father's
story-telling hands were the swoop of owls.

For now, clenched over steering wheels,
knuckles are still, and young faces,

lulled by the engine's hum, slip into sleep
and miss first light spreading in the east.

Making double time, a trucker hauls lumber
on the other side of the highway,

eyes wedged open on amphetamines.
His hand surfaces briefly from the dark cab,

flicks a cigarette. The brilliant cherry shatters
on the asphalt into a thousand sparks

and, at one jump, a thousand ashes.

The Survivalist

My father-in-law and I stand
in the Mosquito River sweating
inside our waders,
the cool current
swirling around our legs.
Mid-July sun cooks the afternoon,
too hot to fish, but we fish.
We have just three days.

Later, just before dusk,
we walk down a two-track road
and check his tree stand.
He points through the branches
to an old shack. It leans—
gravity stronger than the rusted nails,
boards fading back to wood.

A survivalist built that place
my father-in-law says. *Came out here
to live alone. Nobody told him
he had to treat the wood. He canned
his own meat — muskrat, I think.
Used to walk over when we were up
for deer season, said he could see
our lights through the trees.*

He wore camouflage, talked for
 hours.
Two years ago, a DNR officer,
heard a rumor about illegal traps,
stumbled across this place and found
the body thawing on the bed.
 Sometimes
the winters up here just don't end.

A sign planted in the shoulder reads:
Seasonal road, not snowplowed.
I ask my father-in-law:
They're just old logging
 routes.
When the cutting's done, the men
 leave
behind miles of stumps and dying
 roads.
He points to the edge
where the grass and brush spread
out slowly over the scattered dirt.
Some of the lumber they cut
still stands in houses in Detroit.

The next morning a heavy rainstorm
muddies the local rivers
and washes feed in off the banks.
It pours all day, and we don't fish.

Downstate, on Saturdays like this,
my wife and I drive to the big
    bookstore,
thumb through thousands of words,
wait for the waitress to refill our
    coffees.
Up north, we don't even have a
    radio.
We come to escape the noise.
When it rains, we pace the floors.

Sunday, while packing up the truck,
my father-in-law snaps
an inch of siding off our camp.
No fishing next month he says.
We'll have to take a weekend
and paint this place.

Something We Must Face

Where was he going
out of Detroit, speeding north
through thick traffic, leaving
the brick and steel, abandoning
the week's rush of faces?

Why did he follow interstates down
to highways, the ones that fade
into county roads? Unlike city streets,
this pavement's named after nobody,
just letters and numbers.
Soon this drops off into gravel
and leaves behind the community
of yellow dashes and lines.

Would he imagine his escape
seven hours from his driveway
on the seasonal road winding toward camp?
Old joists and walls on the border
of swampland, a family remedy
handed down from his father.

When would he drive the twelve miles
back to the nearest one
street town to buy what he forgot
in his race to arrive?

Eggs, bread, milk, coffee—
a harvest from strange hands.

Didn't he know in the morning,
waking without his wife, he'd hear
the faint moans of a construction
zone? Semis rolling over rumble strips,
the heavy scrape of bulldozers—
county roadmen spreading blacktop

over dirt.

Fishing Weekend, Seven Hours North of Detroit

Though I'd only said it as a joke,
they're still here now,
sleeves rolled or without shirts,
jumping on shovels, extending
themselves into dirt.
Their cars are huddled around my camp,
trunks packed with rods and creels,
but they keep digging.
Christ they say or *Sonuvabitch*
but differently, more the way
I've known them to swear while wading
upstream in deep, fast rivers,
smiles aching in their cheeks.

I bring beers out in the afternoon,
because they're still pitching earth
over their shoulders, determined
to finish this new pit for the outhouse.
They glisten like fish,
Jim jumping out from measuring the depth,
as this two-rut road becomes
the only working neighborhood
left in the state.

Gestures

Past the pulse of taillights
in the ditch, drivers speed home,

toward small-town streets
where they know somebody

and are known. Somewhere in the race
of voiceless lights,

a turn signal blinks
with the rhythm of a handshake.

Snowfall

Over night, a lake effect blizzard
piled snowbanks up above

real estate signs, left nothing
moving until morning and the digging out.

Behind a snow blower, a man carves
a path down his driveway. His son watches

through a window, squints after the familiar
silhouette nearly dissolved in the squalls.

Later, the father stomps his big boots
into the kitchen, his beard heavy with ice.

Lets go, your mom needs milk and bread,
he says, tucking his last cigarette

behind his ear. *Forecast calls for more snow.*
The son gets ready to follow.

* * *

City snowplows, busy exhuming
the main highways, abandon side streets,

and the father steers through the tracks
someone risked at first light.

His son lounges dumbly in the warm breath
of the dashboard, doesn't notice the houses

hunched beneath the heavy snow.
The father edges past a stranded pick-up

wedged into a drift, no driver,
one taillight blinking, mile-long walk

of footprints long since buried.
Two people could have pushed him out,

he says, his words fading with the smoke.
Ahead, the hazy outline of the grocery

store fades in through the whiteout,
but in front, no parking lot, just

high drifts swept across the spaces,
even the wheelchair spots are taken.

* * *

Out in the storm, he and his son run
for the doors but, turning his head

from the cold, the father spots a set
of headlights in the employee parking lot

illuminating nothing. *Battery'll be dead
before his shift ends,* he shouts into the wind

and trudges to the rusted door. He lifts
the handle as though a hand he would kiss.

The dull lights blink off, and he
gently slams the door. Jogging back

to his son, he flicks his cigarette
and the ember, a small flame, begins to thaw

the entombed town before it hisses out.

South Michigan Interstate, Near Detroit

I see the tracks, like two spines
across the snowy shoulder, sloping down
into the median, and then the car

wedged into a drift, silhouette
of a head, like a hand puppet,
loiters above the driver's seat.

I pass two exits and do not turn
around, then remember my father
in the Upper Peninsula, no gloves,

in a Kmart parking lot, jumping
a charge from his truck's battery
to a stranger's stranded Buick.

Twelve years old, then, I watched him,
red knuckled fists clenched
around jumper cables, shoulders stooped

beneath the hood, grounding the negative,
jolting the positive, again and again,
until the rusted four-door turned over.

Like ghosts now, his hands
with frostbitten, open palms
look nothing like my own, warm

and closed over the steering wheel.

Only Birds After All

As though abandoned scraps of night
startled by the rush of morning

headlights, they rise
off thin branches, wind
lifting hollow bones and feathers

into a giant whorl of starlings,
a sudden rorschach
imploding from the stand of trees

rooted in the median.
No driver sees this
from beginning to end.

Some miss how the tiny flicker
of five hundred wings
dissolves inside this mass flight,

how this commune shifts
and cuts through crosswinds.
Speeding toward their own exits,

only a few see how the shape
finally shatters, each darting
for a space among the miles

of telephone wires. They land
apart, shivering and puffing
down in the cold morning light.

A Bus

rolls over old highways
and county roads,
sighs into a station,
then roars on
past factories and silos
until dusk, a changeover stop.
The passengers stretch and eat.

An older driver clocks in
for the dark shift, speaks
into his hand, listens
for warm voices on his CB.
Strangers lean together,
their words flesh out
the silences of the long ride.
Someone borrows aspirin.

All night the driver shields
his eyes against the glare
of oncoming brights,
and the riders count windows
scattered like stars
beyond the shoulders.

Waking tomorrow in the depot,
they'll check their watches
and spread across the city
like a shattered pane of glass.

Road Signs

In the brief sweep of headlights,
trees flicker by like subway faces
and then vanish back to darkness.
In these ways we are deceived:

He notices the branches are losing
leaves, bare limbs against the cold,
and his high beams blink down to dims
for an oncoming windshield,
beauty in the jump of his fingers.

Tornado Warning

Driving under this jaundiced sky,
I'm comforted by the steady voice
announcing on the radio
that the chances end at 7:45.
      I watch the clock
even as the trees go still.
Somewhere someone's gone
to school for this—knows
if wind will twist
into something deadly.
I trust this promise.

A boy on a bike shoots out
from a cross street,
goes through my sight, a brief star,
but here long enough for me
to know he's my son,
      not looking
both ways—reckless.
I turn my head in time
to see his little legs pumping
him toward the darkness
      at the end of the street.

Radio's off.
We can't predict any of this.
Coming through the front door
like a high wind, I huddle my family
into the basement, hold them,
waiting to decide for myself
if the danger has passed.

Below Zero

The weatherman maps out the sources
of another cold snap, another storm.
I envision the small flame inside the furnace,
a blue flicker above a whisper of gas

like my father the morning he drifted
home after a double shift of plowing
county roads and slipped
into the basement to stoke our coals.
Twelve years old, I watched from the bottom step,
his bent silhouette delivering cord wood
out of the blackness into the smoldering embers.
Stomach hollow, he fed the fire
until the room glowed.

Johnny, the snow just wouldn't end he sighed
and then closed the door, disappeared
without forecast, left me grasping
for the banister, eyes unadjusted
to the sudden darkness, until even now,
forty years later, I stumble out of bed,
follow a flashlight down two flights,
and rummage for the owner's manual,
wanting to be ready
in case the pilot light goes out.

My Father
Wrote Short Stories

Twelve years old, my father
found his father, a timber cruiser
wandered in from miles deep
beyond the tree line, fallen
down in the basement, shotgun
shook from his twisted limbs,
twisted the way the Yellow Dog's
last few miles wind desperately
as if trying to dodge the end
where it dwindles into fingers
and fades out through the swale.
Those last downstream miles
just below the 550 bridge
where, at twelve, wading waist deep
next to my father, I witnessed
the nature of darkness and water,
how overcast skies hide our long
shadows, give the trout no sign
of our approach, and how the river
turns through wide bends, pools
beneath fallen logs in dark,
constant eddies, a swallowing gloom
my father swore his father dove
headlong into when the fish
weren't biting. I feared the way

the river rushed me from behind,
bullied me toward the murky pools,
while my father, rooted in the river
bottom, waved his dancing line
above the surface, sweeping
arms casting an incantation, landing
the fly as if the wings were real
and blood pumped through the steel,
barbed thorax. His spell coaxed
a rainbow trout up from the depths,
bursting under the hook, dragging it
down as though trying to pull my father
out of the river bed into the darkness,
swimming deep but losing the fight,
cranked to the edge of the hole
where I waited with the small net.
The silvery body, cradled but thrashing
in the mesh, shined as if its scales reflected
the blaze from my father's tired eyes.
Flying on the high, I rushed downstream
to where the river blackens
through the bottom of a swampy ravine,
but my father called me back, shook
his head, warned me that few trout
are ever worth the darkest waters.

Broken Lamoge

While his son watches
on tiptoes, the father loads
the pellet gun,
using the same small muscles
he'd used the day before
to glue a porcelain rose
to his wife's broken lamoge.
A squirrel slows along the fence,
scratches its ear. The father
hands the weapon to his son.
*The sunflower seeds
aren't for him*, he says,
then drags his finger
across his throat. Winks.
Will the boy ever know
that we are all one pilgrim
of the same hungry journey?
The father grabs the barrel,
shoves it towards the ground.
*How are you going to hit it
with your goddamn eyes closed?*

Pretend Water

In the tender movements of spring, the snow lets fly
its water soul, and farm field gullies and holes
become wishing wells in a child's country.
My father hauled out fishing poles, creel,
hooks and lures, winked to my mother, and we,
brother and I, followed him to those fortnight
trout ponds, our future foxholes for the dry
summer wars.

We would cast the entire day, my brother
on a shovel, jumping to break the wintered soil.
Through eleven Aprils, of course, there was never
a nibble or bite, but if my father could have,
he would have dove down, tugged our lines,
and in an hour prepared us for poetry and God
before we grew away.

Back Casting, Forward Casting

Here where the river eddies
before a windfall,
deepening and widening
into its slow filter through the branches,
I stand behind you,
palm over the back of your hand,
bone guiding bone,
fly rod above us,
needle of a metronome.
I'm showing you rhythm.

Tracing this back to its headwaters,
you're holding my hand
as I steady myself against my first current,
ready to lure rainbows from dark holes.
And this has deeper springs:
your father tucking you in
on beaches, fire-warmed rocks
buried beneath you, a long heat
to take you through the darkness.
And this too goes back through ghosts
of other fathers, like following the water
backwards through gravel and limestone
until soil, rainfall...

In the cabin, unable to name
the weariness that comes before sleep,
my son cries and fights it.
We hear him from the river,
where the one shadow we've been casting
grows long in the setting sun,
and though I know you have the rhythm now,
I'm still not taking my hand from yours,
or the other from your shoulder—letting you,
in the last of this day's light,
teach me how to teach.

Last Cutting Before Snow

in one arm, my infant son
he and I behind the mower

his finger points to the sun
its setting slow, but certain

like the tall, wild grass
collapsing in rows

I let it go too long
I don't mind

that he doesn't know many words
I'd never hear them

above the engine   the leaves
that have fallen become mulch

in a window my wife
watches us for a moment

when we pass again, she's gone
a light comes on in the basement

as he sinks into me, his hand
slips between buttons

settles on my chest, a baby bird
the ache of holding him this way

will burn in my arm tomorrow
his eyes close

Toddler Classes

Waist-deep in the community
pool, I adjust my grip
on my son's slick skin.
We're both here because he's
on the far edge
of eighteen to thirty-six months.
They won't learn to swim
the instructor tells us,
a sweet girl
from the local high school's
swim team, someone's daughter.
We just want them to enjoy
the water. Has her father seen
her lately? What does he
really know anymore?
Sixteen and she's already
directing a shallow end
of shivering adults: *Parents*
blow bubbles, too, she says
or *Hold them behind their necks,*
or *Let them know you're there.*
Front floating above my hands,
my son can't stop smiling.
While the others are only kicking,
he's already groping his arms
into something like a dog paddle.

The instructor floats by,
tells me he's probably ready
for the pre-school classes.
I want to tell her
that I just got here,
that I'd like to stay
for awhile with my fingers
snug between the ripple
of his ribs, my hand nearly
covering his chest.
Above my other palm, though,
I feel the pump and pedal
of his comical little legs.
He's ready, she says again,
and even as I shake
my head, I can feel the way
he sometimes makes the water
work for him, as though,
if I'd ever let go,
he'd start to swim away.

Driving Home from a Niece's Funeral

I stare at the halo
of adhesive on the dashboard

where the plastic statue
of St. Christopher had been

Deer! my wife shouts
a doe glowing ghostly

at the edge of our headlight
we can't even slow before

she flicks an ear then crosses,
a fawn hop-walking behind her

through the predatory light
and back into darkness

we end up on the shoulder
heavily breathing our thankfulness

I check my son's sleeping face
shimmering in the rearview mirror

he fusses against the car's stillness
Probably safe now, my wife whispers

but what I'm sure of anymore is meager
like my high beams in this blackness

my sister had only laid her infant
daughter to bed on her belly

I look at the dark road ahead
and my son disappears

taking my foot from the brake
I begin to mouth the words

of something close to prayer

Alternate Weekend: Eclipse

Moon and sun on cardboard,
shadow of a circle
overshadowing a circle of light,
our son's pinhole projection,
a recollection
of the way we had lived,
filtered and in silhouette,
never risking blindness
to witness how we had crossed
each other,
ritually returning to a darkness
that will not now return to light.

She Chose to Wade

In late October, good swimmers fall
into Lake Superior and freeze
into their drowning.
Anxious college boys,
in the spirit of tribes,
dive from the Black Rocks
into her cold and shout their names
to the world.

My mother, instead, waited
until early spring,
just after her graduation,
when half a degree keeps the water
from going back to ice.
From the beach in South Marquette,
she chose to wade.
With her back to us
she became sexless,
hips beneath the surface.

My dad and I watched from the sand.
Far past the break wall, a long resource
boat, heavy with iron ore, seemed frozen,
until my dad pointed out the distance
between it and the lighthouse growing.
Mom dipped her arms to the wrist,

slowly to the elbow,
then to the shoulder.

I asked my father how steel could float,
but he only sighed, *Isn't she beautiful?*
His hand holding my fingers shook
as though preparing dice for a throw.
What was being gambled?
She dropped slowly to her knees
into blurry visions of blossomed clams,
and when she rose
from the water dripping, she
turned and returned
a reborn she, the pronoun
Adam gave wonders prior to Eve.

Survival Tactics

The fire the men kindled
now owns them—
it's the only way they know
to hold off the darkness.
Huddled, they pass around facts
like ladles of stew,
talking about steel or engines or
capsizing...
Since the first fire,
they've been learning the lines,
passing them down:
Wet clothes are a dead weight.
They'll pull you right under
the grandfather says, feeding cordwood
into the dying embers.
The others nod.

As though smoke, she rises
away from the flames,
drifts down to the beach
where the waves,
drawn by something unseen, pulse
at the sand on this windless evening.
The small breakers hish
where she stands alone,
without words,

staring into the darkness,
ready to swim or even drown
if anything happens to the tiny light
that marks the prow
where her son
is night fishing for trout.

Reprieve

Pond like a palm lifts us,
my father and I in our canoe,
a hand of sky cups over us,
the way we are taught to handle
small, frightened animals.
I feel good, even joyous
despite everything that's been
reported, everything that seems to say
that everything is ending.
He tells me to look
at the heron rising from the rushes,
so labored in its gray takeoff.
Like it I too am suspended,
the air generous today
even for those with so much
stacked against their flight.
I picture my wife at home
holding our infant daughter up.
We chose to have a child
in the shadow of more fear
than we've ever known.
It must have been on a day
such as this—a day for conceiving.
My father strokes and we glide
farther than his effort deserves.
Even the surface is generous.

I think he too feels light.
Wind carries his voice to my back,
stories of his childhood, good
fishing trips with his father.
But even as I hear the smile
in his talking, I watch the way
he keeps us from the far end
where the rotted husks of trees,
like dark memories, tower
from the water, threatening to fall
and crash through the surface
of the perception of everything
we're feeling today.

Up into the Light

All other lights are out.
I sit in the wavering

glow of the television.
Outside, intermittent, cars

stop at the corner,
drivers just silhouettes

in the dashboard light.
They roll through the intersection

out of my sight. What I know
of them is their fading hum.

Everything seems to be flickering,
a candle losing oxygen. Lately,

I can't catch my breath.
Even with the sound low

I don't miss any news,
words tickering across the screen

below the anchor. The way I sit
here—silent, absorbed—

is nothing like prayer, something
I haven't done in years. It's easy now

to think it's all for nothing.
Then there's a rumple of air

from upstairs, the vulgar sound
a ketchup bottle might make

and my wife and son begin giggling
in the afterglow of his flatulence.

I can't help it, I laugh with them,
then take the stairs

two at a time towards the light
shining out of our bedroom.

Sundown

As though marking time,
fly rods swing
above the gray-haired men.
Their eyes adjust slowly
to the fading light.

Late season nymphs emerge,
mayflies drying into first flight.
Having clung to the stony river bottom,
the insects linger above the water,
mourning a mother
that now would drown them.

Standing against the strong current,
the men pause
to watch fingerling trout,
small rainbows breaking the surface,
foolish with hunger and life.

When bats skip low
across the river, the men recall
wristing roofing shingles
in a vacant lot. *It's really not
that dark*, one says.

A mayfly's tiny legs
tangle briefly in his eyelashes.

Back at the tents, neither talks
of sleep. One follows a flashlight,
searches for kindling.
The other, finding a match,
scrapes a flame out of stone.

Losing Work

A wormy apple dangles
in my face.
My son stares up,
maybe catching glimpses
of me through the branches.
Daddy, don't fall, he calls.
Too late, I think.
I don't know why I climbed.
Maybe to impress him.
I really hate heights.
In my parents' basement,
my wife unpacks our clothes
into the dresser I used
as a teen. The basement.
Once my bedroom,
then the spare room and now,
I suppose, my bedroom again.
Our bedroom. The three of us.
I'd hate to think
what she's thinking.
The branches around me are thin,
and I can't remember the hand
or footholds I used to get here.
I hug the trunk. Lost.
Someone opens the sliding glass door.
Mommy, I think daddy's stuck.

Nothing. Then her voice.
He'll be fine, she says, *help me.*
She begins to gather into a pail
bruised, fallen apples.
Yucky, my son complains.
They're good for pies, she says.
When the bucket's full,
she sends him inside.
Then, without scolding,
she begins to talk me down.
Your left foot. Keep reaching.
Feel it? It's a solid branch.
Now with your right hand…
And so on. Branch by branch,
limb gingerly finding limb,
I follow her voice
toward the roots.

Summer Shutdowns

send thousands north,
speeding, trailers weighed down
with everything
they've taken
into this exodus
from the droning
assembly lines,
rising up I-75
like mercury.
The August heat
triggers sudden hatches
of white mayflies,
nymphs unfurled into wings,
cocky stunt pilots
careening, spiraling, flying
too low or disappearing
into the sky
as though still remembering
the undercurrent, the dark rush
always at them,
sweeping some away,
leaving most clinging
to anything,
the safety under stones.
Even in these early hours,
they can feel their wings

tiring, withering.
They must return
to the river.
Their wild flight
suggests they know this,
as though they can sense
the few weeks they have
to live.

Breakdown

The roadside is shivering
with thousands of them,
caddis flies just hatched
from the surface
of some nearby water,
and you're no longer thinking
about the distance to service stations.

You, down on both knees,
spread your fingers into them,
set your palm flat
into the gravel,
feel their legs catch
against the fine hair of your hand.

You can hear them, too,
dying on the highway,
snapping faintly under the tires.
Their closed wings
remind you of hands in prayer.
You will witness this only once.

Behind you cars ticker by
like stock prices
across the bottom of a newscast.

How it happens

is the driver in front
of you lingers
for one second
after the light turns green,
and your hand lunges
for the horn,
smothers it
into its self-centered noise

it feels so good
so right,
this angry
little frustrated orgasm,
but the car ahead
is not nudged
from its daydream
into motion

the driver shifts
into park,
opens his door
and your hand shrinks
like those half-friends
who goad us
into bar fights
and then disappear

when the guy dismounts
his stool
into a magnitude
like that outside your window now
tapping, telling you
to just open up
for one second
in a voice dangerously calm

Flotsam and Jetsam

A man drifts by
in the midstream current
of the Saginaw River
out almost fifty yards
past my bobber.
He's wearing a shirt and tie.

Though he doesn't shout
or thrash his arms
a small part of me
feels responsible for his life.

There are things I could do.
I have a cell phone,
a car, two arms, legs.
I could drive ahead of him,
try to get a boat.
I could dive in.
I could shout, "Are you okay?"

I'm not without options.
But when my bobber vanishes
and my drag squeals
the only thing I can think
is Walleye. Big one, too.

Of course, it's another bullhead.
Twisting pliers into its puckered mouth,
I remember the lone swimmer, the drifter.
I can't see him downstream,
but I tell myself he swam for shore.

The Other

Your tattered tent
is no longer
a tent – scraps, poles,
stakes lost in the ground.
The food you carried
here was gone weeks ago.
The sun has not come
up in days. You came
here to escape,
to be by yourself,
and now you are alone.
The last flames
of your last log
flicker in the embers.
Your eyes adjust
slowly to the blackness.
Another fire smolders
across the meadow,
another silhouette
standing, craning
a neck towards you.
You each wave, hands
like surrendering flags,
and though the distance
and darkness mask
the other's face,

you jog, then run
across the field
as though drawn
to someone you've loved
for a long time,
as though the face
you expect to find
will be your own.

Opening

You hold a can of ravioli
in the dream, but no opener.
Someone calls you
towards a doorway, says
something about a hacksaw.
The face of the stranger
fades in, becoming
your own, as are the hands
now sawing through the tin.
The stranger wears clothes
from a bag you brought
to Goodwill a month ago.
Chow down the stranger says,
a phrase you often use.
Finishing, you lick cold
sauce from your fingers.
Heaven on earth the stranger
sighs, and you fight like hell
to keep from waking.

Green

Wanting to sell our house,
my wife and I agreed
against methylene chloride's
bleed into the ground water,
and so with the first door up
on saw horses, I poured
eco-friendly paint stripper,
remembering our realtor
advising, *People want natural
wood in Victorian homes.*

After six applications,
faint swatches of oak
faded up through the layers,
giving me time to imagine
the twelve other doors.
We wanted better neighbors,
central air, a bigger yard,
and needed to be on the market
before the end of March.
*Most houses sell in April
and May,* our realtor said.

The second can of stripper
annihilated the years of paint,
bubbling up globs of acid mucous

to fly from my scraper, smoldering
to yellow the spring grass
around my blue tarp, leaving
my fingertips and knuckles
simmering like the upper arms
of old men having heart attacks.

My wife and I didn't talk
about the first can of stripper
we abandoned in the garage
of that house we no longer own.
They loved your woodwork,
the realtor congratulated,
and our house sold immediately
and for more than we'd hoped,
which we agreed in the end
was really the important thing.

Clean

Her small body shines
with water and light.
Giggling, she squeals *daddy*,
splashes until his pants darken.
Five more minutes, he thinks,
stepping out quickly,
pouring himself a drink,
not expecting to return
to find her slipped under,
her tiny face staring up
through the undulating surface.
Before he can move,
or drop his scotch,
she raises her dripping head,
her mouth a perfect O.
The sound of her gulped breath
takes the wind out of him.
Her face, pale and awed,
understands the other side
of water and air.
His wife didn't see,
doesn't know.
Her feet pulse and fade
in the upstairs joists.
His daughter cries,
slips from him, not giggling.

She wants out.
He tries to keep her
in the tub, in the light.
He's on his knees.

Sleep Over

It's the first time
he doesn't want us
around. They disappear
upstairs with sleeping bags,
pillows, a miniature suitcase,
like bonsai luggage.
They close the door.
My wife and I aren't sure
what to do with our
sudden personal space.
We drift around
the empty downstairs.
I go to the landing
twice, lift a foot
to the first step.
My wife shakes her head.
Just let them play,
she says, smiling,
watching the weather
channel, trying to be positive
despite the cold fronts.
The upstairs rumbles
with their running
and distant voices.
What they will begin
to share tonight in whispers

will leave us behind,
the start of what will be
our son's own life.
Watching TV, my wife
and I remember
how to hold hands
like teenagers. Skin
finds skin, fingers
slide between fingers,
knotting, intertwining,
palms sweating
beneath the slow rhythm
of thumb rubbing thumb
until coming
downstairs so quietly,
they startle us,
as though we'd forgotten
we weren't alone.

Blood Work
for Ken Meisel

Daddy, where are you going?
he whispers, pajamas glowing.
I kneel down, tell him
I need to have blood drawn.
His brow furrows.
Should I mention
that the doctor said
it could be nothing?
He looks behind me
where my wife is sleeping.
That's been our fight lately,
keeping him in his own bed.
Go on. Go ahead, I say,
understanding his longing
to crawl into her arms.
He disappears into the doorway.
My car's heater blows cold air,
houses and streets still dark.
Alarms haven't gone off yet.
Just need to be sure, the doctor said.
That evening, in the backyard,
I toss a football to my son.
At work, the guys saw my bandage,
the gauze with its spot of blood.
A letter's always better

than a phone call, one says.
He's had his scares.
My son crouches over the ball.
If it turns up something,
the doctor said, *we'll go from there.*
I'm going long, my son says,
a phrase I taught him. He snaps
the ball, takes off like hell,
the way his memory
could eventually lose me
until I'm something
he can barely make out
in the darkness behind him.
His tiny silhouette crosses
into the next yard, the next.
I track his distance by the light
he runs through, swatches
from windows and glass doors.
My wife's blond hair
moves in our own window,
hovering above the stove.
I have no appetite.
Daddy, I'm open, he shouts.
Hit me in the numbers!
He absorbs every word I say,
makes me want to go long.
Night comes so early anymore.
Dad! he yells, his voice

different now, pleading.
I don't even know
if I can get it that far.
I put up a Hail Mary pass
into the settled darkness,
the kind we used to throw
when we were kids,
and we were behind,
and still desperate
for some kind of chance
to stay in the game.

Another Man Admires
My Wife's Cups

No, nothing like that.
In our kitchen. Coffee cups.
My wife hung them
from small golden hooks
she twisted into the wood
beneath the cupboards.

The guy says he likes the line
of the cups, how they hold
the room together.
He's a mathematician, sees
things I can't see. My wife
complained just last week
that I don't like anything.

Mr. Math dates Susan,
formerly of TomandSusan,
my best friend's ex-wife.

The mathematician joins
the couples in the living room,
where other marriages
could be dying. *I always
liked your cups,* I say, grinning.

My wife doesn't laugh, leaves me
alone in the kitchen.

I study the cups.
Why not just put them away?
Why this small trick, this flare?
Why the work?

Tom must know why
I couldn't invite him. I joked
to my wife that it might
make things more interesting.

Tom probably wonders
how it all fell apart.
Maybe he's looking at a doorknob
right now, waiting for it
to turn, for things to return,
having no idea, as I'm just
starting to see, that every union
dangles from a small hook,
tries to fill the emptiness of coffee cups,
to make a true line
that holds everything together.

What We Have

We lie in the flickering light
of the silenced television,
our son between us, not
a bridge, but a furnace
of fever heating our fears.
We've seen the news
and know how an illness
can become suddenly lethal,
like a stiff neck missed
as a sign of Meningitis.
Pumping my thumb
through the channels,
I find nothing to turn
our minds from where
they go on such nights,
when every thought returns
to the sorrows we have
ahead of us, the decline
or vanishing of each love,
the late-night phone call
or some other breaking
of the news, like my mother
whispering into the receiver
last autumn about my father,
an MRI, nodules, and lungs.
One day into seven months
of nursing him, and her words

were already mostly medical.
She learned a new language
only to witness his slipping
anyway into hospice,
the way the channels
disappear one into the other
until I find the film *Duck Soup*.
Imagine these four Jews
lampooning the idiocy of war,
like they could already see
the jigsaw piles of bodies.
1933 – Mussolini, Hitler,
and this scene with Groucho
and Margaret Dumont,
the society woman who played
it straight to Marx's one-liners.
Her character tells Groucho's
that she was with her husband
to the end, and he replies,
No wonder he passed away.
Dumont despised the brothers
and their off-screen pranks,
yet I have to believe she stayed
for more than just the money,
that she'd heard the audiences
howling, releasing the Depression,
like us waking our sweaty son
for the peanut vendor scene,
the silent slap-stick sight gags

one after the other
until finally Harpo is pedaling
his filthy legs through his rival's
lemonade, and a tiny giggle
grows between us, and we join
it until we are laughing too
hard for any kind of coughing
or fever or the threat
of anything yet to come.

Stripped

Six years old, I heard my father thump down the stairs,
witnessed him — naked, dripping, a fleshy blur
running between me and the Zenith Chromacolor
patting my head or maybe using me for balance
as he made the slippery turn toward the kitchen
and my mother going pale at the stovetop, shouting
his first name and with it her shock, her laughter
and maybe her own understanding of everything
he was feeling, loving his watery footprints still
on her linoleum and the hum of his quick kiss
in her cheek and his other cheeks finally gone
upstairs to the bathroom where they belonged
covered again and then him later walking down,
leaving as usual for his job, as I will soon
though it's thirty years after and I'm at my sink
in the bathroom of a house I somehow own,
remembering that morning my father streaked
and hearing my children just outside this door,
my daughter sobbing and my son trying to handle
the world like a man, announcing *It's nothing
to cry about* like he's talking to me and the way
I suddenly feel, standing in my underwear, sizing
up my body that's lost the hardness of my twenties
and knowing how they'll look at me when I turn
the knob, as though I deserve their confidence,
unaware that I'm terrified of what it means to have
them and how everything could easily fall apart

and it would be my fault because I never bothered
to really study what it was I was getting myself into
and I guess I'm feeling my own urge to disclose
for my family that I am only just like them, a child
wanting to feel the abandon of running naked
and fearless, though still hoping for someone
to pick me up, whisper that things will be okay,
and so what I really need after all is my father
to tell me why his wasn't a retreat, but a victory
lap, a momentary celebration of everything he had
to lose, everything that scared him senseless
and made everything else make sense, and I guess
with him gone now it has to be enough to know
that he'd had such a morning of certainty and joy
and it is this that I have to try to remember
as I pull on my clothes and open the door.

Jeff Vande Zande

Epiphany

Many mornings it strikes
me that I could be
a better father, a better husband.
I could be a better man.
It presents itself so logically.

Usually I'm on the toilet,
poised symbolically
to expunge everything
that somehow conspired
to make me someone
I sometimes loathe,
like when I say something
to my wife and then think,
Shut up, Jeff, shut up.
When did I get to be
so impatient, so insensitive,
so damn negative?

It seems simple, really.
Just be a better person.
Say what they need to hear.
Do the things they need done.
They have their past too,
and it's left them with holes.
We are what we were.
It's not like I don't know

the words, the actions
that could make things lovelier.

And so I flush, and close
the lid, and replace the roll
and wash my hands.
I find my wife in the kitchen
and tell her what I've thought—
that her jogging every other day
is paying off and she just looks
incredible, and she stuns me.

You want sex tonight, don't you?
she says, and I know that's not why
I said it, but her smile tells me
I just might get some, and who am I
to ignore an epiphany's fringe benefits?

It's only a minute later
(seven minutes since I became
a better man) that she says
we should take the kids
to the Detroit Zoo, and I argue,
The zoo? Really? I don't know.
It's so much driving, so much work.
No. No, let's not today.
Forty bucks? No thanks.

It's my mother's penny-pinching,
in my genes like heart disease,
and my father's absolute dread
of anything sprung, unexpected,
that has us here again
angry with each other.

The rest of the day I'm no better
man than I was the day before.
We don't go to the zoo.
I yell at my daughter once
because I'm frustrated
about something else.
I do some good here and there,
but looking at myself from outside
is still pretty disappointing.

I have the epiphany most mornings,
and I guess there's something
in that, and it seems pretty easy,
really, to decide to be someone
other than who I've been,
and there's tomorrow, and maybe
I'll last eight minutes.
Or, at the very least, seven again.